A Strong And Fragile Thing

Musings in reflection of the wisdom and wonder found in the natural world.

Lauren Lott

For Dad and Mum.

Copyright © 2021 Lauren Lott
All rights reserved.
No part of this book may be used, reproduced or resold
in any form without written permission from the author.
ISBN: 978-0-6489466-4-9

If the rose does not know,
ask the clouds.
If they too are unsure,
go to the river and listen.
If the river does not speak,
wait for a breeze, or a storm,
a sunset or a shallow-tail butterfly.
It won't be long before you find
what is hidden; sooner or later,
earth or sky, water or weather,
will speak to you.

07
SKY WINKS

57
EARTH BODIES

107
WATER FACES

157
WEATHER VOICES

SKY WINKS

Sunrise;
beauty before I begin.

-the way love goes.

She came overhead,
and placed colour before me.
It's only 7am,
and I'm already consuming rainbows.

-but first, wonder.

Billions do not dim
the light of one,
But aren't they astounding
when they shine together.

-the stars and us.

Lauren Lott

The moon man is round tonight;
full and burnished.
Hard to miss.
Hard not to hear.
He only says what he lives,
'Understand you compete with no one.'

Hours,
watching sky change,
witnessing each cloud
cruise overhead.
At first,
I saw only
the slow fold of shapes,
a continuous blend of colour,
until, I sensed
the invaluable privilege of being here.

Lauren Lott

The ordinary
is really something;
a cloud cruising the sky,
a bird cleaning its wings,
a hand held for a short time.
They are all,
and all at once,
real,
common,
enchanting.

We only get
a number of sunsets,
so excuse me when I slow,
I never like to pass up
a seat in the front row.

-never seen before show.

Of course,
the cosmos began with poetry.
That's what love does;
lights up.

-the stanza of stars.

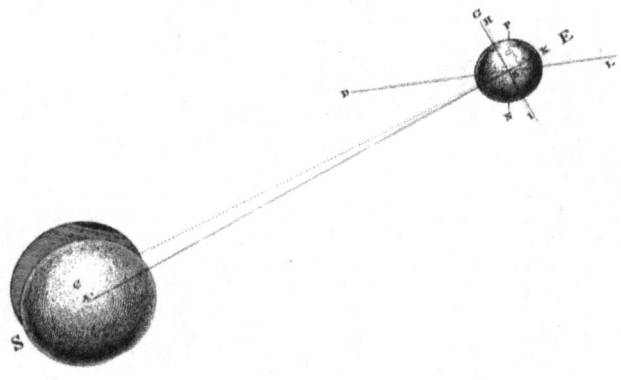

Love is eternally creating.
The universe is continually growing.
And you,
my dear,
are becoming,
forever becoming.

Lauren Lott

He is calm.
I think it's because
from way up there,
He sees it is all coming together.

-mellow yellow moon.

Wait a few days after crying,
after calling out,
and soon you will see
something break through.
An expression unlike you envisioned;
maybe only a cloud the size of your hand,
but still, there will be something.
Something pleasantly,
or uncomfortably
perfect for you.

Lauren Lott

First light,
and my first thoughts
are of days gone by;
a time lived by someone else.

I wonder if noon feels
that way about morning;
same day, different colour sky.
She can't be 7am
no matter how hard she tries.

All she can do
is shine her midday sun,
and know soon
she will fold into twilight.

Although she will change again,
and may feel she no longer shines as bright,
her fading will bring out the stars,
and she will carry a cooling ease,
as serene as the dark blue night.

We own the sky,
but choose to fly together.

You swoop,
I glide.

You soar,
I cruise the current.

We do this
because we know,
to love is to set free,
and to be free,
is to let go
of that which is not love.

Lauren Lott

When all the world
seems like nothing
but dirt,
and stone,
and ash,
I look up.
There is always
a patch of colour
somewhere.

Bright star,
those that stand afar
perceive you are small.

-they don't know you.

Lauren Lott

Content for most
to sleep through
your finest hours,
you teach us to shine,
whether seen or forgotten.

-moon, oh moon.

And what does the sun,
ask of the seed?
Who does she deem it should be?

-no one but itself.

Lauren Lott

She taps my head
with her sunny hand,
showing me I am seen,
and how I can also see others.

It does not matter
that I cannot keep them;
that I cannot hold them forever.

For I hold this moment,
and in doing so,
allow the moment to hold me.
That is all I have and need.

Clouds drip overhead,
waiting not to deliver
what rumbles inside.
We are like them.
Our destiny flows from within,
held not in the hands of another.

Lauren Lott

Open skies, open hearts.

This beautiful night,
I am born with the stars.

As they burn
billions of years away,
I am also alight.

I am dust and sparkle.
I am dirt and shine.

The darkness tells me so.

Wrote moonshine
on water below,
'There is more to life
than what you know.
Keep exploring
the skies,
the seas,
your soul.'

I know you have stories lived,
never told.
Words written
never read.
Tears spilt
never seen.
Feelings felt
never said.
It's alright now.
Use what can not be given away.
Mix tears and dark memories
to make bricks.
Build stairs, not walls;
elevate, don't isolate.
Let all the unseen,
all that goes unsaid,
take you closer to the moon.

As sun warms my head,
I cannot help but feel,
I am being kissed,
crowned,
commissioned.
She seems to say,
'Though I am high,
and you are grounded,
today we both have significant work to do;
the work of warming others,
the work of reminding earth
how beautiful it is to be alive'.

Cold shoulders
invite me
into something
more suited.

-if earth did not turn, we would miss the moon.

Lauren Lott

Let them go.
Let them discover life without you.
Let them see how you are sunshine.
Let them love the dark,
or come looking for brightness.

Winter sun,
takes the weight off,
and warmly asks,
'What is more pressing than love?'

Lauren Lott

Although,
I don't always feel strong,
I believe from sunrise to sunrise,
as I choose love,
I am becoming stronger.

I do not wonder
why this sky, on this night.
Why this body?
Why this face?
Why this life in this place?
I no longer ask why
at all anymore.
Sure, I look for meaning,
but mostly I let life flow,
recording with poetry and pictures,
the story of me,
of us,
of we,
as life unfolds.

-learning to ask more exciting questions.

Dawn.
I'm swimming in soft light,
halfway between waking and dreaming;
somewhere between a warm lull,
and a sting that leads to open skies.
Such favour we have,
to wake and dream each day.

Yesterday called again.
I sat and ate
as she sang her slow twang,
assuming I still like the same music,
spoke the same language.

It was pleasant enough,
but when she left,
I felt my body let go,
and I noticed the night
was thick with stardust.

I have decided,
if she calls again,
I will ask her not to sing,
and together we will listen to the tune of stars.

I am unsure if she will like it,
but she can choose,
to pick a harmony,
or simply not call again.

Lauren Lott

Tell
the
story
that
makes
you
glow.
Freedom
is
in
the
mind
you
know.

-the memoir of stars.

He teaches to love from afar.
See how he passes on light,
without need of being included?
And we,
we can be
just as generous
when they don't invite us in.

-moonnerisms.

Lauren Lott

The universe is
wide in diversity,
explosive with creativity,
abundant in provision -
take from her,
all the inspiration you need,
to become.

-something to do while you're here.

We cannot choose,
when we are born,
or where,
or in which family.
We cannot choose,
who falls in love with us,
or if another will treat us kindly.
We cannot choose,
how many sunsets we see,
or what the wind blows our way.
And so,
we choose what we can,
and in doing so,
prove love to be,
the only thing we need to choose,
to go a good way.

Lauren Lott

I hear them talk about stars,
as though they keep them
in their pockets,
using words too common,
too small,
for that which is so high,
burns so bright.
Maybe they should stop talking,
leave their knowledge,
and look up again at twilight.

-only fools try to frame the sky.

I wish I could tell you,
that the stars will never leave,
and the world will let you sleep,
but that is a tale told by fairies.
You will be shaken;
awakened without warrant or warning.
But fret not;
every calamity brings clarity,
rousing you to see the day.

Winter skies
remind us
there is beauty in the grey;
uncertainty has its own
kind of charm.

I was taught,
to be steadfast
is to be strong.
But those that stand,
do not move.
And those that do not move,
cannot see what the world is like
beyond where they are.
If we cannot see,
how can we understand?
If we cannot understand,
how can we empathise?
And isn't empathy the highest form
of giving and receiving?

-the reason the earth moves around the sun.

Lauren Lott

Some wake to see the sunrise.
I wake to farewell the moon.
For I have learnt to love the dark,
as much as the day.

The moon does not assume.
Though he sees
more than most.
Still,
he gives me
the courtesy to speak,
and by his silence,
shows me what it means
to be heard; wanted for heart.

Lauren Lott

The sun tells
what no one else can.
Feel the words that
have tumbled from her mouth,
land on your skin?
They warm and burn
like only truth can.
That is why we long for her
on cloud choked days,
and run from her
when we'd rather the haze
of untold stories.

Feet on soft grass.
Face to the sun.
Body brushed by breeze.

-what it feels like to be kissed head to toe.

Lauren Lott

With so much space
to be themselves,
they can't help but shine.

-stars and souls alike.

As if by magic,
the sun appears,
bringing with her,
the laugh of birds
and reminding earth,
some things wait in hiding,
until dawn is proclaimed.

Lauren Lott

I am grateful for the light
pulling colours;
dressing up everyday trees,
repainting the same patch of sky,
making art out of it all,
over and over again.

-beautiful is the ordinary in focus.

I find you in rhythm;
it seems you would rather
dance than run.

Often I need to slow down
to catch up to you;
to hurry ahead is to fall behind.

Yes, I find you in rhythm,
swaying in sunlight.
Twirling with time.

-honesty

Lauren Lott

We all hide,
from what we fear,
but it's ok
outside,
I'm here.

-love equals the universe x infinity

EARTH BODIES

I do not often go
to the mountains,
but I know
gratitude and fresh air
feel the same.

Lauren Lott

I see the way
the light caresses leaves,
how the breeze tenderly
plays with river reeds,
and it is clear to me;
we don't need to be heroes.
We just need to
take care of each other.

Though they are cut
and sit in a vase on my table,
they have no trouble blooming;
filling the room with perfume,
drawing the eye with their colour,
teaching us how to go out giving.

Lauren Lott

The bees seem
to hold no prejudice;
whether a garden rose,
or a flower wild,
they happily give and take
declaring every bloom beautiful
and necessary.
And such is love,
hovering over all souls,
validating both the kept
and those left out in the cold.

When I don't feel love,
when I think I lack what I need,
I look up and let the living come to me.
It is then that I see,
I am a part of something wonderful.
Love is abundantly everywhere.
In, around, before and behind.
It comes in many forms;
the smile of a daisy,
the stroke of a summer breeze
the show of swans on the lake.
Often I think too little of love.
Maybe that has been my biggest error.

Lauren Lott

She grows over the water and hangs,
almost kissing the surface.
Discontent only to receive,
she is interested in giving back,
a picture of gratitude;
the most beautiful branch on the tree.

Oh to be transfixed,
undistracted.

To hold your focus.
To give you mine.

Oh to be taken by one bloom,
one petal,
when eyes could wander,
when hearts could want a garden.

Oh to be highly present,
truly grateful,
wildly devoted to what or who
is right in front of us.

Lauren Lott

I noticed the butterflies
you sent me,
and the promises
you left on my door step.
I heard others echo what
you whispered to my heart.
Coincidence?
Or madness?
Or maybe you come to me
in many ways.

Didn't love burst open?
Doesn't us mean everyone?
Isn't earth a kind of heaven,
if we believe we have enough?
Are not arms meant for holding?
Are not hearts made to feel?
Isn't today as good as tomorrow,
if love is all that is real?

Lauren Lott

As the creeping fig reaches,
she teaches.
I write down her gentle instruction.
'Love aligns,
and creativity is the key
to becoming unstuck'.

Of this we can be confident:
healthy things grow.
Like the crabapple tree
covered in springtime kisses,
good things flourish.

Hope sounds like the birds.
When I listen,
I hear the message in their song.
'Wake up.
There are so many colours out here.
Do not miss the morning
by thinking about the night.'

I put stomach to earth
and whisper,
'I will be with you one day.
On a day as ordinary as this,
we will become one,
and we will both be stronger for it.'
Ashes to ashes.
Spirit free of shell.

Lauren Lott

What is living if not learning,
growing,
transforming?

Is it not the vision of all
to reach a seasoned age
with storerooms of sweet memories?

Do we not all dream
of the delicious reality
of being
truly,
wholly,
freely
ourselves?

-the hope in every seed.

I love the way the birds
always seem to know
what to say in the morning.
I think they understand
the miracle of a new day;
that every sunrise is special.

Lauren Lott

And what will you choose today?
To sit with the dandelions?
To stand with the tall pine?
To let branches cradle your body?
Or will you pass by
wisdom,
wonder,
beauty,
without hearing one word
they have to say to you.
If healing is to be found,
surely it is amongst the renewed.

I expected them all
to bud the same colour,
but there on one stem
a peculiar sight,
one pink,
one white.
Those sweet lilies
reminded me,
I live in a world of
strange happenings,
unpredictable turnings,
and there beside the vase
my heart flowered with possibility.

Lauren Lott

Maybe,
the best thing
we can do
for each other
is surrender to
our own blooming.

I do not think
there is anything sweeter
than the harmonious
alignment of spirits;
the way his branches hold her,
as she sings to him.

Lauren Lott

I see you in the most peculiar places;
on the frame of the bathroom mirror,
resting on line hung linin,
circling in near darkness
hours after midnight.
I can't help but feel
like you have been sent to me.
Maybe you are a seen whisper,
a kiss blown from invisible lips,
the future come to confirm my path.

-the language of butterflies.

The trees know how to be.
They do not rush after birds,
begging them to rest in their branches.
They are grounded,
seemingly content to be themselves.
Too wise to chase after flighty things.

Lauren Lott

Maybe we should be
more like the fairy moth.

-gentle with ourselves.

I love early morning
when I can hear
the coo of pigeons
on the eve outside my window.
It is there,
in those moments,
I feel held,
much like I hold my china cup:
full palm,
thumb,
four fingers.
I believe,
love has got a good grip on me.

She waves as if to say,
'look closer, take notes.'
And so I lean in and see
all her doing is growth.
She multiplies through connection.
She is busy with nothing but love.

-lessons from a lime tree.

Trees bowed low,
heavy with growth,
show me how to be thankful
for both sun and rain.

Lauren Lott

Maybe we shouldn't
tell them to shoot for the stars,
not to wish to be
ballerinas or firefighters,
astronauts or doctors.

Maybe we should tell them
to aim for the earth instead.
To focus on being green.
Healthy and whole.
Someone who never stops growing.

Maybe we should show them
how to be in love with being alive.

Didn't you feel your heart bloom
when she said those freedom words?
Didn't you feel your chest rise
when she recited her daybreak verse?
Didn't you want to join her?
Didn't you wish your words could whip like that,
sing like that,
shine like the side of her sword?
Didn't you, if not for one wild moment,
want to reach up and grab
a corner of the curtain she holds
and help pull it back.
Didn't you see,
if not for the first time,
your power,
our gleaming future,
the possible end to this fight?

Have you noticed
they rise with feathers;
fragile, feeble things.
Maybe we too could turn
our weakness into wings.

A Strong and Fragile Thing

There are times I feel
I have nothing to say,
and I can't think of a reason
others should listen to me.
But then I hear the mynah bird sing,
and I think,
if a creature as small as he,
has the audacity to open his beak,
calling to whomever is
still enough to listen,
then maybe my words
will resonate with
someone,
somewhere,
and one is all I need
to keep me from being silent.

-someone needs to hear what you have to say.

Lauren Lott

To breathe deep and slow.
To release wants
and surrender outcomes.
To love others and yourself.
This is freedom.
This is how we open our wings.

The silky oak does not
battle the seasons.
It seems it has resolved,
if summer will not fight for it,
it will not fight for summer.

Lauren Lott

They do not care to ask.
They think they cannot learn
from such a small thing;
from those who do not
sit around boardroom tables.
This is the error of most,
for I have found wisdom
in the mouth of young creatures,
and new wine on the lips of the outcast.

Spiders in the trees,
making magic,
busy with fragile things.
But what else is a spider to do?
What is a spider without a web?
What is a heart without expression?
What is a day if not taken in?
What is a life if not poured out
in love for others?

Lauren Lott

The oak wears its hearts on its sleeves.
Hundreds of acorns
put out for the world to see.

And just like these hard cupule nuts,
our hearts do not open with ease.

They crack.
They split.
They break.
They burst in pain.
They drop with weight.

But in time we see.
There is no other way
for the heart to be free.

Surrender, never said I.
Until I heard the cackle of a kookaburra,
and saw that surrender is how
this free one flies.
For daily he gives in to laughter,
and the impulse to go high.

Lauren Lott

I do not understand
the bird who night after night
sleeps in the same tree,
cooing the same chorus.
She has no law to bind her.
She needs not years to raise her young.
When there is so much sky,
with little time to dream beneath the sun,
why sit so long on familiar branches?

Try not to miss a thing;
the orange tipped wing butterfly,
the song of the wren,
the kiss of spring rain,
the parade of the waterhen.
Take it all in,
no need to fix a thing.
Be here, bear witness.
Relax and bring it in.

Lauren Lott

The vine will find a way;
gates and garden walls,
fences and fish ponds
will not stop it.
It seems to see chaos
as the cue to create,
every obstacle
an opportunity to explore.
I want to be more like that.

Now I see why the path winds;
why it twists and bends and loops.
There are lessons hidden in the belly of the oak,
and wisdom lays unburied where fresh water
strokes the shore.
There are omens budding between
thorns and wild roses,
and healing is crouched in the crag
of salt-crusted rocks.
Bashfully, creativity creeps to drink at the stream,
and beneath the low black plum branches,
new hope is born.
Yes, I see why the path winds,
for what is life without
lessons,
wisdom,
omens,
healing,
creativity
and new hope.

Like the wild rose
she is too sharp for vases,
too sprawling for boxes.
She thrives in secret valleys,
heartily enduring.
Yes, you will see her grow
in unexpected places.

Light on leaves.

-heaven's kind hello.

If you are uninvited,
remember,
there is a place for you.
A place to grow,
to mature,
to multiply,
to become a forest.
Life always has others in mind;
your place of exile,
a spacious home
for those to come.

Unlike the seed,
we have many chances to grow.
If this town,
this job,
this relationship,
does not nourish,
and we cannot push down roots,
or grow sweet fruit,
we can replant in richer soil.

-grow where you grow/stay where you bloom.

Lauren Lott

You can't see it,
but the seed is broken.
More than what you 'hope will be',
already born.
It will grow,
and become its own tree;
inflorescence never bloomed before.
Expect something beautiful,
but understand,
you have not seen it,
so you cannot know it until it buds.

When my soul is dry,
I walk twenty minutes from home,
and sit on a stump by the water.
While I rest there,
I remind myself that we,
the stump and I,
are alike.
We live long after we are cut off.
Though we seem barren,
there is life within us.

Lauren Lott

And there in the glow of dawn,
when I felt all had turned their backs,
I stood before glass,
and saw a forest of branches
pointing at my body,
directing prayers,
reaching to hold my heart.

-earth angels.

There is a garden in my chest.
Sweet peas pop up from a bed of peace.

Though I live not in the Mediterranean,
they are native to me.

For it is known,
these beauties are given in thankfulness,
and thankfulness flowers in me.

Lauren Lott

Baby leaves,
bunched in clusters.
Some will be eaten by insects.
Some torn by birds.
Some shaken down by children
swinging on low branches,
or blown beyond the yard
by more than a breeze.
The lucky ones will last till autumn.
They will know what it feels like
to wear seasonal gowns,
green,
yellow,
orange,
brown.
All will be gone by winter;
once time decides the new must come.

WATER FACES

I am learning
the language of waves;
the rush in,
the pull back,
the high swell,
the humble retreat.

Surely we too,
made of sand and water,
move the same.

We are pushed forward
purposed to kiss the earth,
before disappearing into
the unfathomable.

Lauren Lott

If you'll be like water,
unbound by your present plight,
you'll seep out from the smallest crack,
you'll be as free as light.

If you'll be rock-like,
unsurrended to the flow,
you'll be trapped,
held hostage,
by what you think you know.

The sea is kind to me.
See the way she washes sand,
painting over prints,
erasing where I stumbled.

It seems she is more interested in me,
than the mark I leave.
I wish people were more like that.

Lauren Lott

Learn from the ocean;
go deep,
stretch wide,
sparkle under light.

See the way,
strong winds throw,
the ocean forward?
See how it whips,
giving water wings,
making curls out of chaos?

And you also,
with the weather at your back,
can be moved quickly towards the shore,
apart from your doing.

-spirit work.

When I was unwelcomed at the riverside,
and pushed into the wild,
I found a well just for me.
While others tasted
what comes from the sky,
I drank what is drawn from the deep.

-there is enough for you.

We are like the waves.

Some gladly dump themselves
at the foot of the shore,
exhausted from the
wash and churn and tumble.

Some ride tall,
pulled up by invisible hands,
going further than others,
fortunate to be born when the tide is high.

Still all only travel as far as life allows;
we are at the mercy of what is beyond us.

Lauren Lott

When I look at her full body,
I can not help but feel like
there are treasures for me within her depths,
and if I stay here long enough,
if I make her shores my home,
one day, those treasures will wash up at my feet.

-sticking with love.

As I walk the sandy corridor,
I hear you
before I see you.

I breathe you
before I bathe in your belly.

If earth was a body,
you would be the soul;
the part we are supposed
to fall in love with,
over, and over again.

Lauren Lott

Mother sea,
you be how mothers be,
birthing not once
but constantly,
stirring life inside of me.

Take it in,
without need of putting words to it,
or finding meaning.

Let the ocean be large.
The sunlight - beautiful.
The sea birds - playful.

And you,
let yourself be here.
That is enough.
Just as it is, it is all enough.

Lauren Lott

I have come to breathe slow,
here where the water laps,
and my shadow lays on broken shells.

And as I seek selah,
I feel myself mend,
becoming whole,
although,
I intend on staying a little broken.

For then I was broken in,
and now,
I have broken free.

Though daily
we may not make big moves,
and indeed at times feel stuck,
in truth, we are going places.

Like the river,
tranquil yet travelling on,
rolling softly,
the motion of our lives,
the depth of our love,
is proved by beginnings and ends.

Days on.
I remember how
my head was low,
and my eyes made
pools on terracotta tiles.
No one could see me,
but I was fulfilling destiny.
I was on my way.

Birds play in the pool.
The sound of their wings on water
reminds me to nourish myself.
Wash.
Cleanse.
Move.
Feed.
Nurture.
Care.

-sacred rituals.

Face in sunlight.
Feet in sand.
I have come to drop and bury pain;
to let the rhythm of waves
resuscitate me again.

And in return,
I feed her tears,
making her fuller.
We, the ocean and me,
know how to take care of each other.

Maybe roads
should be forged
more than followed,
rivers crossed
more than cruised.
mountains climbed
more than charted,
love shown more than said.

Though with you
I sense my smallness,
I always feel larger when I leave.
Your big brings out the big in me.

-ocean advances.

We all have a river within,
moving us towards the things
true to our soul.

-swim with the stream.

Though she shines,
on the surface,
on her skin,
oh the bounty,
that lives within.

-ocean girl.

It is hard letting you decide,
I am afraid you will not see the dangers.
And to be honest,
I wish you'd ask me.

For to ask is to affirm
that I am worthy of being followed.

As the years go by,
and I am less needed,
I am learning how to manage
the fear of being less wanted.

-when the river becomes two streams.

Lauren Lott

You are light,
when worries
weigh on your body.
You flow easy,
when faced with hard things.
You are a twig on the river,
a dandelion on the wind,
content to let love decide where you land.

I hope when your body
folds into the ocean,
her body slips into your soul,
and you return home
with a roar in your heart,
and rise to be true, free and whole.

Lauren Lott

On champagne shores,
she bathes my toes,
and bubbles under my feet.
It seems she is always in celebration.
Hear how she tells
a grand and glorious story,
'It is good,'
'It is good,'
even when I insist on believing it is not.

-I'm starting to see it her way.

I am as sure as the shore;
changing as waves question me,
proving me right and wrong tidally,
entreating I live openly.

Take her at her word,
listen,
with each wave
she exhorts,
live,
live,
live.

-truly, wholly, freely.

See the way
the river stills,
allowing what is good
to land in her lap.

-vessel of light.

The sea has permission to be messy.
Branches rarely grow straight.
The eagle glides in erroneous circles.
The sun sets both early and late.

And we too,
a part of this masterpiece,
faulter when we try to live neat.

So go wide,
stretch high little wildling,
twist, and sprawl, and accrete.

Thank you.

-all I can say when I see the ocean.

Lauren Lott

She is practiced,
proficient in the art
of giving and getting.
Maybe that is why
she is full and far-reaching;
lacking nothing.

-see the sea.

Do you hear her benediction
as it billows towards your body.
'Peace.
Peace.
Peace be yours.'
I hope you do not resist.

-lakeside.

'What are you afraid of?'
She often asks me questions
when I am looking for answers.
I think she knows
truth folds fear,
opens hearts,
frees spirits.

-said sea to me.

There she is,
showing me how to quiet
my thoughts and feelings,
and live from the deep place.

-the abyssal approach.

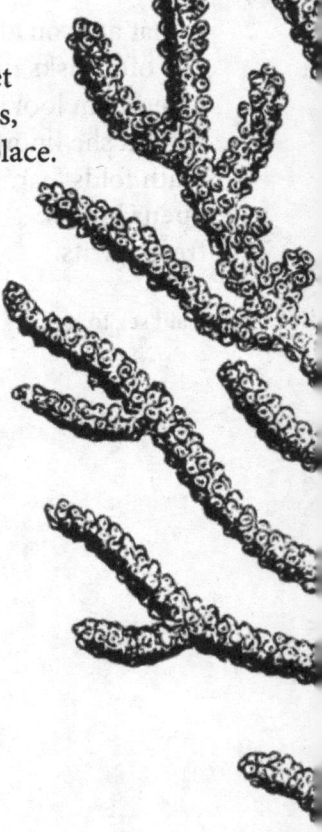

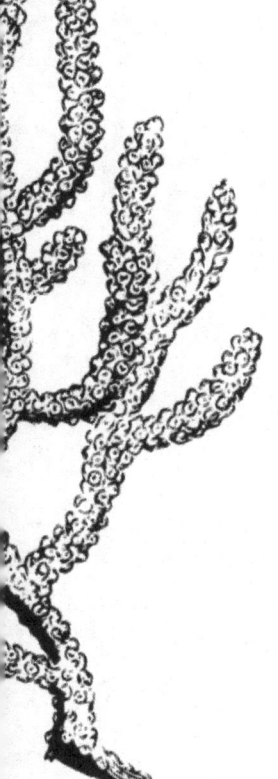

It seems she is busy
with nothing but
being glorious.

-deep blue behavior.

The sea at sunset.

-poetry that cannot be penned.

Quietly,
she reminds me,
everything comes and goes.

-tide talk.

As I surrender and drift
with the rise and fall
of changing waters,
I am learning
the power of being present,
truly here.

-where joy lives.

We decide what we see;
wrechedness or possibility.

-shipwrecked or a survivor.

I have crossed seas
since the last time you saw me.
I have wandered deserts,
and descended valleys deep.
And now a woodland thrives between us;
it's growth, not grievances that apart we keep.

Everyone feels it,
when their feet leave the sand,
when they trust the water to hold them,
and the tide takes them in its hand.
Weightless.
Unburdened.
Free.

-an invitation to surrender.

Sea turns sand to silk,
smoothing out grains,
whitewashing wounds,
daring to push further every time.

And we too,
can be embalmed
like the shore,
if we let love.

Oceanic.

-the truth of us.

She tells a story,
a narrative about love
that I'm choosing to believe.

-infinite blue

And maybe she is also here,
to show us what love is like;
too vast to take her all in,
too large to keep anyone out.

-enough for everyone.

New tide,
here to churn the deep,
bringing sunken dreams
to the surface.

If it wasn't for this disruption,
they would have dissolved completely.

Each breath
is a beginning.

Every blink,
the start of something new.

There are first times everywhere
and in everything, we say and do.

-swimming in a sea of second chances.

Over time,
I have grown
to emulate her;
I want to be
as refreshing as she.

Heart open.
Meditations, deep.
Work, far reaching.
Presence, healing.
You could say,
she reminds me
of the kind of human
I want to be.

So I'll continue
to go to the ocean.
I'm hoping she rubs off on me.

Lauren Lott

She is always,
in the right place,
at the right time,
because
she is,
wildly,
where she is.

See the way,
her waves fold
with intention,
dreaming not
to fall
on another shore.

WEATHER VOICES

Good morning light.
I see you behind closed blinds,
ready to kiss
the foot of my bed,
and baptize me
in a new day.

You hold me sacred,
even before my feet
touch the floor,
for I,
like all,
house the breath of love.

And I am,
like all things living,
a marvel.

Lauren Lott

She pushes,
we sway.

I think she knows,
we cannot see,
what we need to see,
unless we move.

Clever is the bitter gale
that changes our view.

I have always loved
the sound of thunder,
the way the sky
tells me I am small;
a whisper in the world.

If I am small,
I need only do small things;
shake a hand,
smile at a stranger,
help a sister up.

I can leave it to thunder
to shake the earth.

It is hard to leave you
on rainy days.
I don't know if it's because
your branches droop,
or how your leaves
appear a truer shade of green,
but I see the way
raindrops humble you,
And to me,
humility is the most beautiful quality of all.

'Seventy two.'
That's what he said.
'There are seventy-two seasons,
in the traditional Japanese calendar.

One.
East wind melts ice.

Two.
Bush warblers start singing.

Three.
Fish emerge from ice.'

As he spoke,
I felt my heart tip forward,
wanting to fall.

'Four.
Rain moistens soil.

Five.
Mist starts to linger.

Six.
Grass sprouts. Trees bud.'

And fall it did.
But not far before words
turned into heart wings.

'Seven.
Hibernating insects surface.

Eight.
First peach blossoms.

Nine.
Caterpillars become butterflies.'

I asked him about September.
'In which season was I born?'

He asked me for a number.
And when I said 'Eight'
a sweet smile formed on his face.

'Forty Three.
Dew glistens white on grass.'

I don't know if it is possible
to be in love with time,
but there,
listening to him,
I had never been so astonished
by what it does,
or so grateful
that things don't come
all at once.

I remember,
as a child,
staring out at lights
on the horizon,
hope-filled and wondering.
Now, many years later,
I want to be there for that girl;
I want to show her,
she let the rain
ripen her golden.

Lauren Lott

I caught it at noonday,
a sense of coming change.

It seemed the season slightly shuffled
its winter body back,
and rolled over into springtime.

I love how time transforms gently,
gifting us miles and milestones,
seasons and segues equal in beauty.

Every tree,
animal,
bird and insect.
Every season,
storm,
star and cloud,
seem to say the same thing.

-you are here to let go.

This day,
take in all
the beautiful things;
shapes and colours,
forms and fragrances,
melodies and harmonies,
textures and tastes.
It's all for you.
It's all for you.

An experiential artist,
she works with time,
sculpting seasons
for our delight.

-experiential light.

I woke up hungry,
looking for you
in subtle light.

There isn't a good day
that I didn't see you;
in the distance,
or somewhere
deep inside of me.

-hope.

What you perceive as death,
may just be winter.

When it's misty,
focus on the light
clipped frosted glass,
and worry not
about what can't be seen
beyond the pane.

-surviving winter.

I sat watching,
a long time
and then
suddenly,
bullets from the sky,
enthusiastically
plunging into dirt,
holding nothing back.

This is devotion,
is it not?
The way sky gives to earth,
over, and over again.

Lauren Lott

Peace like morning rain,
softening the earth of my heart,
soaking deep,
showing me that although
we live in a world full of heartaches,
generous healing flows,
kissing first the head,
before bathing the body delicately,
like water pearls love the petals on a rose.

And just like that,
the southerly blows through,
and breathes into still heat,
taking minutes to wrestle
the temperature down below forty.

We have been waiting days for
this wild turning,
this cool healing,
this sudden relief.

Oh how she loves
to teach us to trust.

Lauren Lott

Midday storm.
You speak.
I wake,
to secrets within.

-now I see.

There is nothing like
the smell of morning;
the way a new day
feels in your lungs.
Light fades up
and in through windows
whispering,
'See now- you can start again.'

Misty mornings.

-magic from the moment we wake up.

She shows me
how to let go
without giving up;
She wants,
but is not
ruled by wanting.

-she believes in seasons.

Lauren Lott

When I wish for no memory
of harm said,
or harm done,
the night reminds me
to paint with light;
Love always brings the sparkle.

Dawn crouches like a friend,
poised to surprise
on your birthday.
Although her hooray fades in,
I get the feeling
she can't wait to see your delight
when you realise she's here
in celebration of you.

Have you noticed
the sky when it storms?
An assortment of purples and greys.
A water and light display.
A theatrical cloud parade.
Re-enchantment always arrives with the rain.

Be still,
and you will see,
We are all made of
the same thing.

-spirit wind.

Lauren Lott

Soon winter will let go,
though there will
always be hints of it;
the coat hung in the wardrobe,
the blankets folded in the chest
at the end of the bed,
the unlit fireplace swept of ashes.
Though we don't always perceive it,
warmth is ready long before the cold calls again.

Rainy Saturday,
I'm glad I can sit with you,
watching how your presence
changes everything.
Seeing first hand,
the power generosity has
to awaken earth.
All are included.
You fall on weeds and roses alike.
Both the swan and the snake drink you in.
Rainy Saturday,
you show us that all belong.

Lauren Lott

Morning knocks
on my window.
I lift the latch
and let her in.
Mercy,
mercy,
mercy,
spills into the room
and gets all over me.

We've got two sets of eyes.
One set is in the heart,
to see through the storm,
to see in the dark.

They said,
'You've changed.'
 I answered,
'It's called transformation –
the living can't help it.'

As you get older,
I hope you become braver.
What else is ageing for,
if not to dare to do
what frightened youth dream.

-what night creatures know.

Lauren Lott

I write in raindrops,
catching poems,
drip by drip,
drinking dreams,
sip by sip.

-progress needs patience.

Dress sagged low, dripping.
Hair stuck to face, clinging.
Mud on feet,
on ankles,
on knees.
I am found in blinding sleet,
in showers of grief.
But, it is you,
oh storm,
who is new on the scene.
It is you who has never encountered me.
I'm at home in these hills.
I know where to step,
and when to stand,
where to climb,
and when to bow.
You will, in time,
sail away, or fade to empty.
And I, will see sunshine.

Lauren Lott

All voices,
popular opinions,
cultural norms,
can not size up to a small beetle,
metallic in colour.
Not even one raindrop resting on a leaf.

For when it comes to wisdom,
nature glows best.
She is the fount from which
free hearts drink;
the temple where wild ones worship.
She teaches them not to mistake
comfort for freedom,
culture for truth,
attachment for connection.

They listen,
and with every breath
become more and more alive.

Authenticity.

-oxygen

Lauren Lott

Rain falls from my eyes
every time I think
of where I've been,
what I've seen,
and how history has brought me here.

-I found my heart miles from where I thought I should be.

Sometimes,
I want it to rain,
but it doesn't.

-learning to love what makes me move outside.

Lauren Lott

She blows in.
Have you noticed
how she cares not to
talk of trivial things,
like where she's from,
or how long she'll stay?
Have you noticed
whether she whistles sharply,
or whispers softly,
she speaks not of what floats in her head,
but what swims in her soul?

These spring days,
when afternoons stretch out
over hours of sky gazing,
and sun lazing.
We find ourselves
grateful for cool water,
and the simple pleasure
of witnessing colour
not yet seen this year;
the pop of new green,
the prance of bud red,
the puff of purple fountain grass.
This is the season that hope is seen everywhere,
and we bring it into our hearts.

Lauren Lott

And I noticed the honeyed day
laid open before me
matched my place of heart,
and my state of mind.

-happy.

If you walk slow,
you might hear a
beating beneath the snow.

Something thought dead,
still living.

Something thought lost,
lying in wait.

Something released,
returning.

But if you do not hear it,
do not become low,
for if not rebirth,
then soon new birth,
deep beneath the snow.

Although I am dark with pain,
and deep in grief,
by letting go,
you did me a great kindness.

-said winter to the warmer months.

Afternoon,
whether the work is done or not,
you are easy on me.
Needing no explanation,
you seem to say,
'You are here, and it is good.'

Lauren Lott

Love lights a million candles,
and sets the hills aflame.
Love is the sun and the moon,
the wind,
the earth,
the rain.
Love stands before today,
in tomorrow's hopeful light.
Love remains behind the hour,
in yesterday's lonely night.

Boundless love

-the forecast.

Wind,
making waves,
crafting curls,
giving each height and momentum.

I cannot help but feel
that it is also true of us,
that we are shaped by the unseen,
for some kind of purpose.

-everyone of us

Also by Lauren Lott

The Remains of Burning.

Special Thanks

My Family. Thank you for being patient with me as I follow my heart. To Lotty for making sense of techy things.

Islam Farid. You are a talent. I am yet to meet anyone who can visually interpret the heart of a project like you.

Glen and Emma. For your time, encouragemnt, creative input, and honest feedback, thank you.

You, dear reader. For your attention and trust. I hope these poems remind you, we are here to unfold.

Hi,

It's Lauren.

I hope you enjoyed 'A Strong and Fragile Thing'.

Which poem is your favourite?

I'd love to know what you think of the book. An honest review would be appreciated.

There is nothing more exciting to me than seeing my words in the wild! If you post about 'A Strong and Fragile Thing' on your socials, don't forget to tag me! It would honestly make my day.

love and more love
xx

LOVE - MAIL

Head over to www.lauren-lott.com
to sign up for my monthly newsletter filled with
new poems, first to know news on
freebies, upcoming creative projects,
and fun giveaways.

Follow me on

Instagram - @llott.writes
Tik Tok - @llott.writes
Facebook - @llott.writes

Lauren Lott is the author of two inspirational poetry books.

In October 2020, Lauren's first collection 'The Remains of Burning,' debuted on Amazon as the #1 New Release in Australian Poetry. Her second collection, 'A Strong and Fragile Thing', was published in June 2021.

As a writer, poet and certified therapeutic writing couch, Lauren seeks to heal, enliven and ignite wonder and curiosity through language.

Throughout her life, Lauren has actively been involved in many creative projects,
taking on roles such as events creative director, performing artist, speaker, blogger/content writer and florist.

She believes the most rewarding life is gained when she makes space to practice mindfulness and creativity.

Lauren lives in Lake Macquarie, Australia with her family.

www.ingramcontent.com/pod-product-compliance
Lightning Source LLC
Chambersburg PA
CBHW010245010526
44107CB00063B/2690